PIANO / VOCAL / GUITAR

CHRISTMAS

MW01180657

WITHDRAWN

ISBN 978-1-4234-8000-6

HAL•LEONARD®
CORPORATION

7777 W. BLUEMOUND RD. P.O. BOX 13819 MILWAUKEE, WI 53213

Visit Hal Leonard Online at
www.halleonard.com

ALL I REALLY WANT

Words and Music by
STEVEN CURTIS CHAPMAN

Steady four

Well, I don't know _ if you _ re - mem - ber me or not;

I'm one of the kids _ they brought in from _ the home. _

And from ev-'ry-thing _ I've heard, _ it sounds like the great-est gift _ on earth _ would be _____ a mom. All I real-ly want _ for Christ - mas _____ is some-one who'll _ be here _ to sing me "Hap - py Birth - day" for the next ___ one hun - dred years. _ And it's o - kay _

D.S. al Coda

CODA

BELIEVE
from Warner Bros. Pictures' THE POLAR EXPRESS

Words and Music by GLEN BALLARD
and ALAN SILVESTRI

15

ALL IS WELL TONIGHT

Words and Music by TINA CLARK,
GARY PRIM and CECE WINANS

BORN IN BETHLEHEM

Words and Music by MAC POWELL, DAVID CARR,
TAI ANDERSON, BRAD AVERY and MARK LEE

Joyously, in 2

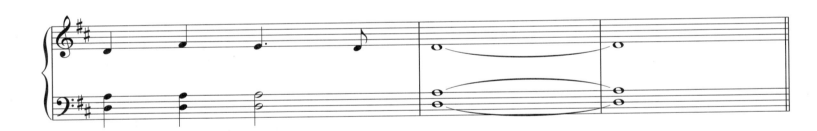

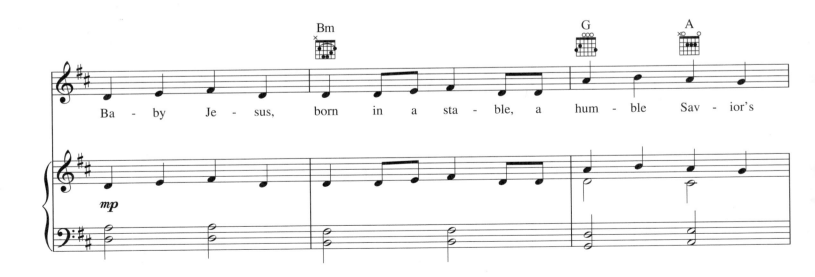

Ba - by Je - sus, born in a sta - ble, a hum - ble Sav - ior's

Born in Beth - le - hem.

BREATH OF HEAVEN
(Mary's Song)

Words and Music by AMY GRANT
and CHRIS EATON

CODA

CHILD OF PEACE

Words and Music by
BOB FARRELL

Flowing

JESU, JOY OF MAN'S DESIRING (J.S. Bach)

On a night of _____

CHRISTMAS ANGELS

Words and Music by JONAS MYRIN
and MICHAEL W. SMITH

CHRISTMAS TIME IS HERE

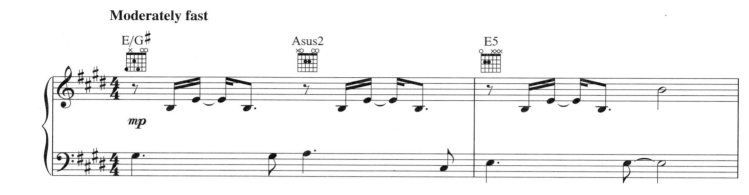

Words and Music by JASON INGRAM
and BEBO NORMAN

Moderately fast

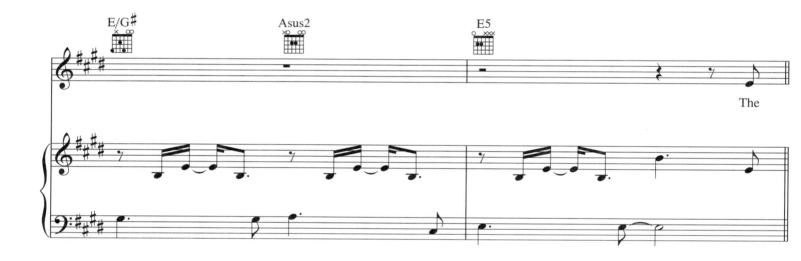

The

days   are   get   -   ting   cold;   it's
smell   of   ev   -   er   -   green,   a
for   a   mo   -   ment   now,   let's

52

CHRISTMAS OFFERING

Words and Music by
PAUL BALOCHE

EMMANUEL

Words and Music by JANIS IAN
and KYE FLEMING

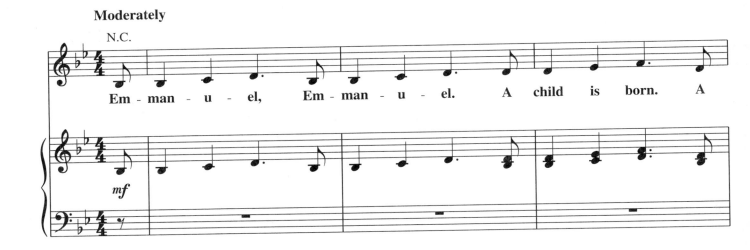

This can be sung as a 3 part round, with the 2nd and 3rd voices entering at these places.

EMMANUEL, GOD WITH US

Words and Music by CHRIS EATON,
ROBERT MARSHALL and AMY GRANT

GROWN-UP CHRISTMAS LIST

Words and Music by DAVID FOSTER
and LINDA THOMPSON-JENNER

FsusF

I HEARD THE BELLS ON CHRISTMAS DAY

Words by HENRY WADSWORTH LONGFELLOW
Additional Words and Music by MARK HALL
and DALE OLIVER

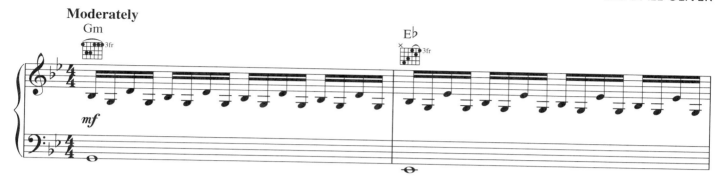

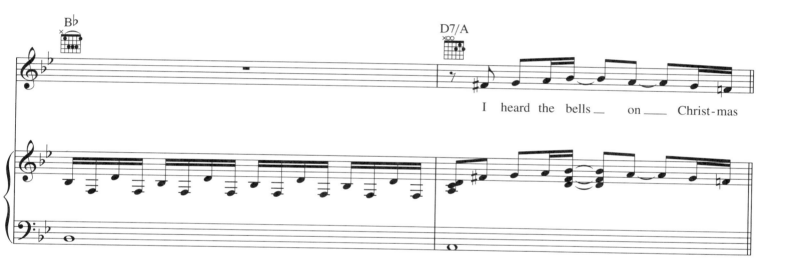

I heard the bells __ on __ Christ-mas

day,
head:

their old __ fa - mil - iar car - ols
"There is __ no peace __ on earth," I

HE MADE A WAY IN A MANGER

Words and Music by LEE BLACK
and STEVE MERKEL

Long - ing for ___ a Sav - ior, ___ a
Beth - le - hem, ___ a sta - ble be -

hope - less world ___ would wait. ___ Sin de - mand - ed jus - tice at a
came a throne ___ of grace, ___ as God Him - self, ___ our Sav - ior, drew ___

I NEED A SILENT NIGHT

Words and Music by CHRIS EATON
and AMY GRANT

si - lent night, ___ a ho - ly night, ___ to

hear an an - gel voice ___ through the cha - os and ___ the noise. ___

I need a mid - night clear, ___ a lit - tle peace right here, ___

To Coda

___ to end ___ this cra - zy day ___ with a si - lent ___ night.

JESUS BORN ON THIS DAY

Words and Music by MARIAH CAREY
and WALTER AFANASIEFF

*Vocal harmony 2nd time only.

THE LAST CHRISTMAS WITHOUT YOU

Words and Music by STEVE HINDALONG
and MATT SLOCUM

I feel your heart beat-ing in-

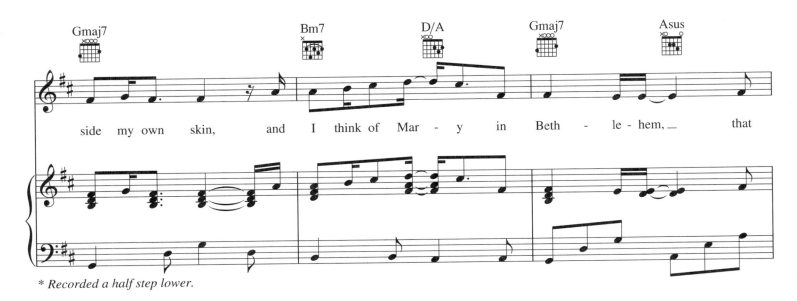

side my own skin, and I think of Mar-y in Beth-le-hem,__ that

Recorded a half step lower.

MESSIAH HAS COME

Words and Music by MARC BYRD
and STEVE HINDALONG

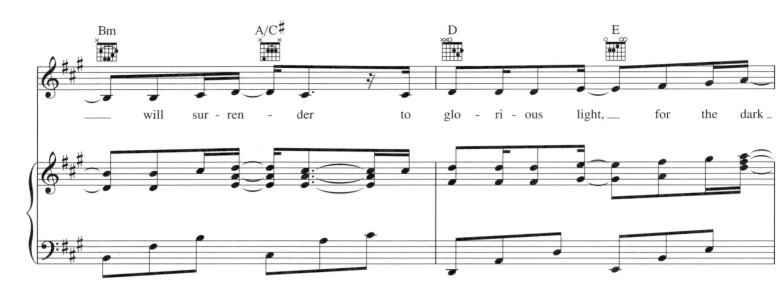

_____ will sur - ren - der to glo - ri - ous light, ___ for the dark ___

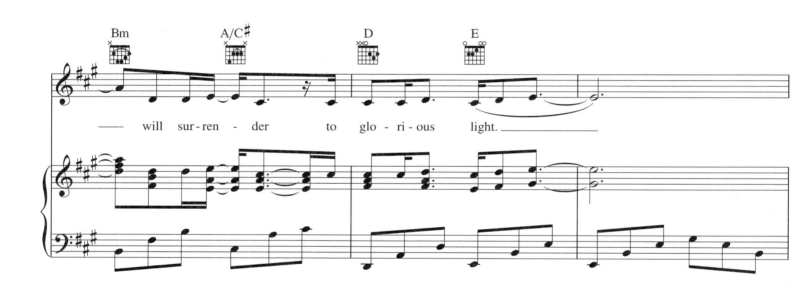

_____ will sur - ren - der to glo - ri - ous light. _____

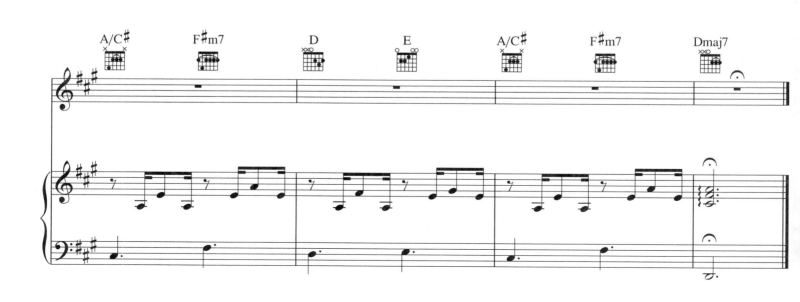

JOY TO THE WORLD
(A Christmas Prayer)

Words and Music by KEVIN JONAS, SR.
and NICHOLAS JONAS

*Recorded a half step higher.

PART OF HEAVEN

Words and Music by THOM SCHUYLER
and CRAIG BICKHARDT

He's part __ of heav - en.

PEACE

Words and Music by MICHAEL McDONALD
and BETH NIELSEN CHAPMAN

Solemnly, rubato

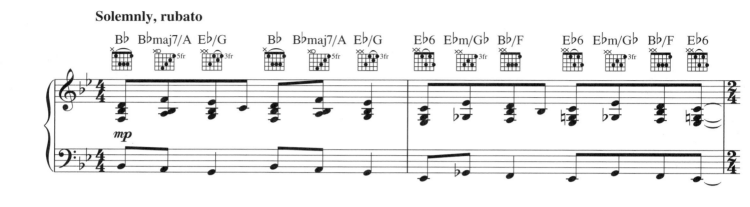

I have come from so far a - way, ___ down the
longed through these wast - ed years ___ to out -
Child of whom the an - gels sing, ___ know my

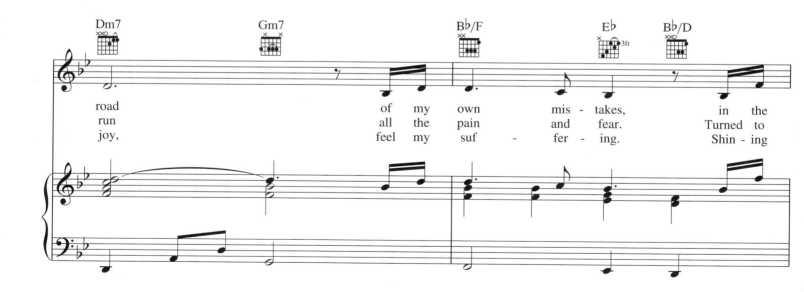

road of my own mis - takes, in the
run all the pain and fear. Turned to
joy, feel my suf - fer - ing. Shin - ing

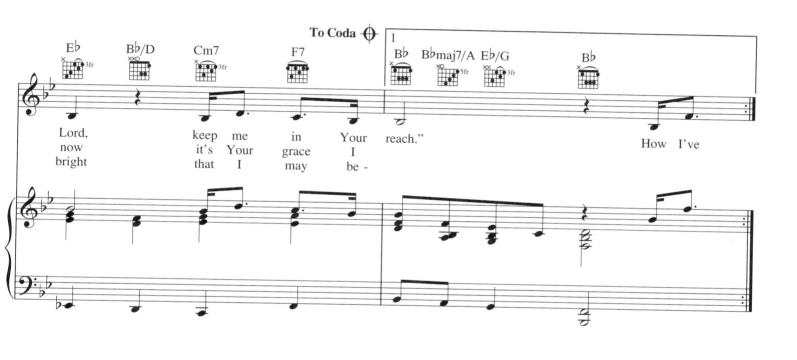

131

A REASON FOR THE SEASON

Words and Music by PAUL NELSON,
RICHIE McDONALD and LARRY BOONE

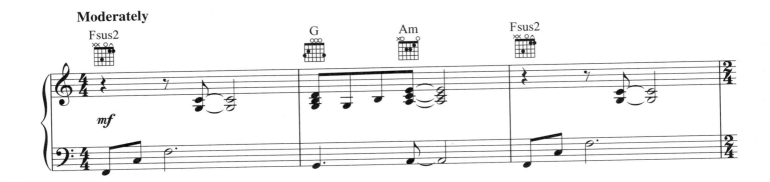

The shep-herds are led ___ by a

star in the sky. ___ On the out-skirts of town ___ a new ba-by cries. ___ No

of this time.

He is ___ the,

THE STAR STILL SHINES

Words and Music by JOHN COLGIN,
MICHAEL PURYEAR and DON POYTHRESS

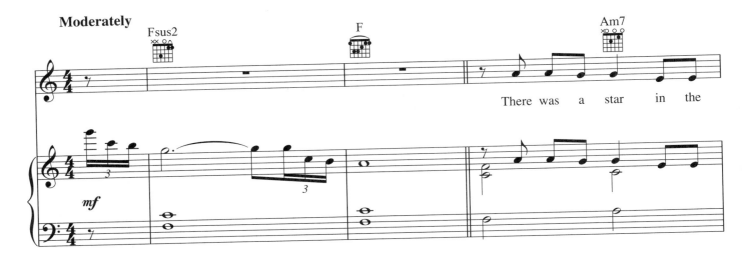

There was a star in the

East-ern sky ___ shown down on Beth-le-hem. ___

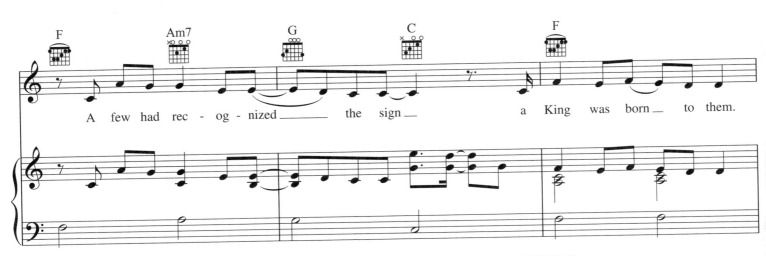

A few had rec-og-nized ___ the sign ___ a King was born ___ to them.

The star still

shines.

Optional Ending

Repeat and Fade

THANKFUL

Words and Music by CAROLE BAYER SAGER,
DAVID FOSTER and RICHARD PAGE

* Recorded a half step higher.

So for to - night, we pray for

what we know can be. _____ And on this day, we

hope for what we still can't see. It's up to

THIS IS CHRISTMAS

Words and Music by
GINNY OWENS

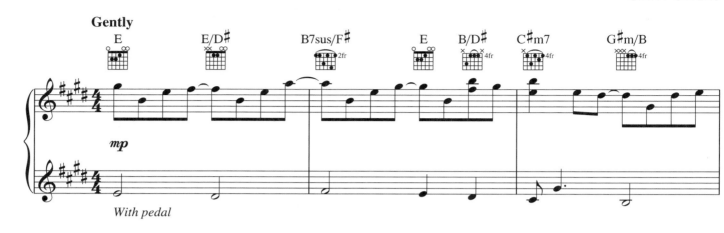

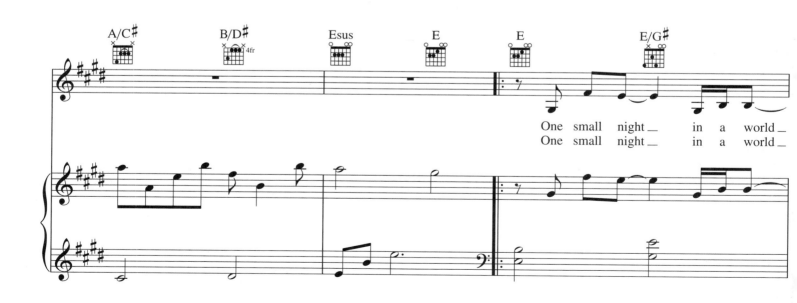

One small night ___ in a world ___
One small night ___ in a world ___

us, ___

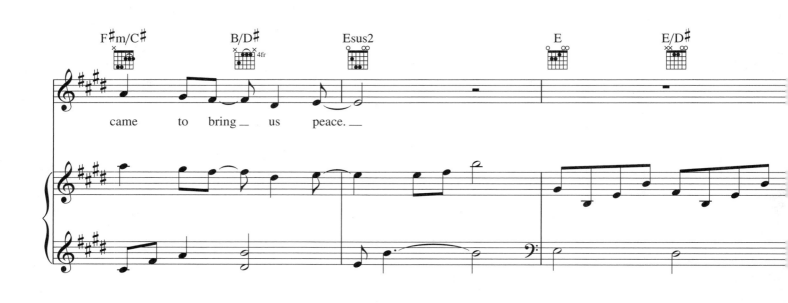

came   to   bring ___ us   peace. ___

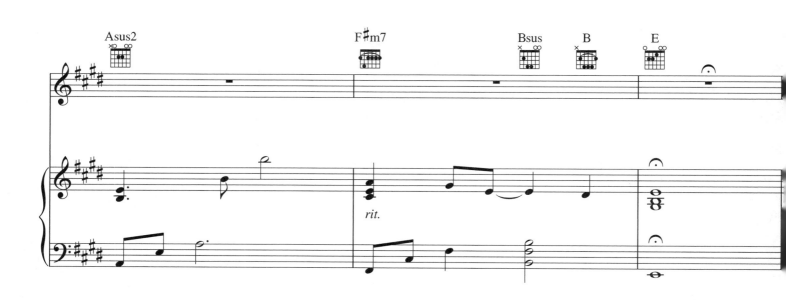

rit.

TENNESSEE CHRISTMAS

Words and Music by AMY GRANT
and GARY CHAPMAN

Moderate 4

With pedal

Come on weath- er- man give us ___ a fore-
Ev- 'ry now ___ and then ___ I get ___ a wan-

-cast snow- y white. ___
-derin' urge ___ to see,

Can't you hear ___ the prayers ___ of ev- 'ry child ___
may- be Cal- i- for- nia, may- be Tin-

WANDERING PILGRIM

Words and Music by
TWILA PARIS

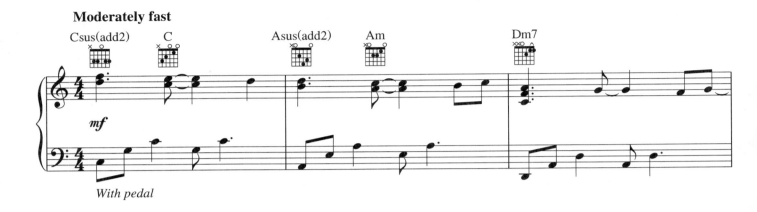

Moderately fast

With pedal

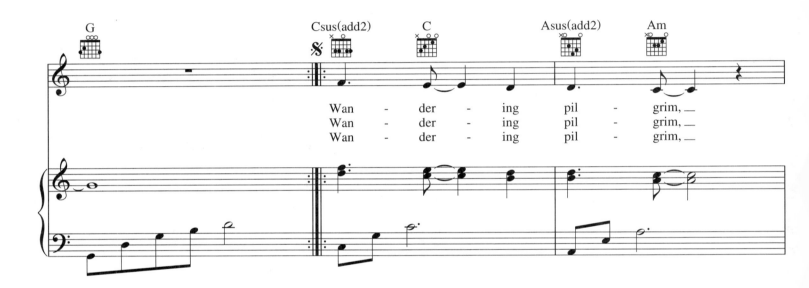

Wan - der - ing pil - grim, ___
Wan - der - ing pil - grim, ___
Wan - der - ing pil - grim, ___

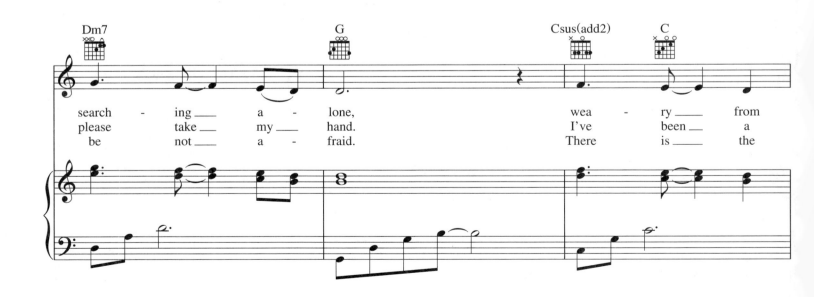

search - ing ___ a - lone, wea - ry ___ from
please take ___ my ___ hand. I've been ___ a
be not ___ a - fraid. There is ___ the

show you ___ the star. _____

Fol - low ___ that won - der - ful star. _____

WHAT A WONDERFUL BEGINNING

Words and Music by AUSTIN CUNNINGHAM
and ALLEN SHAMBLIN

WHEN LOVE CAME DOWN

Written by CHRIS EATO

WHO WOULD IMAGINE A KING

from the Touchstone Motion Picture THE PREACHER'S WIFE

Words and Music by MERVYN WARREN
and HALLERIN HILTON HILL

Gentle Waltz

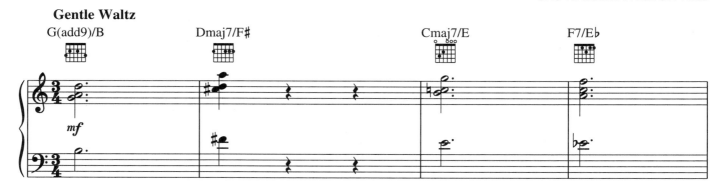

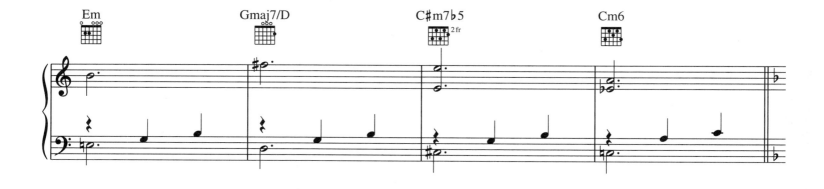

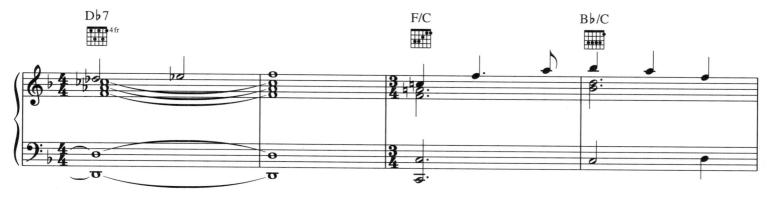